# A FOREST'S LIFE

## From Meadow to Mature Woodland

CATHY MANIA
AND ROBERT MANIA

**A First Book**

Franklin Watts
A Division of Grolier Publishing
New York • London • Hong Kong • Sydney
Danbury, Connecticut

Cover design by Steve Scott
Book design by Molly Heron
Illustration created by Stewart Graphics.

Note to Readers: Terms defined in the glossary are *italicized* in the text.

Photographs ©: Cathy Mania: 7, 10, 16, 19, 28, 29, 44; Comstock: 51; Donald J. Leopold: cover, 6, 9, 17, 20, 22, 24, 26, 31, 34, 36, 37, 39, 43, 49; James C. Smalley: 12; Photo Researchers: 46 (Gregory G. Dimijian, M.D.), 47 (Kenneth W. Fink), 32 (Tom McHugh), 14 (Jim Steinberg); Visuals Unlimited: 53 (Walt Anderson).

Library of Congress Cataloging-in-Publication Data

Mania, Cathy
    A forest's life: from meadow to mature woodland / Robert C. Mania, Jr. and Cathy Mania
    p.   cm. — (A First book)
    Includes bibliographical references and index.
    Summary: Introduces forests, including information about the broadleaf forest, the intermediate forest, and plants that are found in forests. The final chapter has simple activities for readers to do.
    ISBN 0-531-20297-6 (lib. bdg.) 0-531-15878-0 (pbk.)
    1. Forest ecology—Juvenile literature. 2. Forests and forestry—Juvenile literature.
3. Plant succession—Juvenile literature.   [1. Forests and forestry. 2. Forest ecology.
   3. Ecology.]    I. Mania, Cathy.   II. Title.   III. Series.
QK938.F6M24    1997
577.3—dc21                                            96-37286
                                                         CIP
                                                         AC

# CONTENTS

# CHAPTER
## 1
## INSIDE THE FOREST

Have you ever walked through a forest? Did you miss the noise of televisions and radios and cars and trucks? The forest is very different from areas where people live. It is darker, cooler, and filled with its own strange noises. Is it any wonder that people once thought of the forest as a magical place where elves, pixies, and fairies lived?

Eventually, people overcame their awe of the forest. They began to use trees and other forest plants. They cut down the trees to build homes and keep their fires going. They learned to use roots and berries to color fabric and treat illnesses.

Although people have relied on forests for centuries, only recently have we realized how important they are for our survival. Did you know that about 30 percent of the earth's surface is covered by forests? In

A forest is cool, dark, and quiet because the leaves of the tall trees absorb heat, light, and noise.

fact, 40 percent of North America is forested. Although we use wood from forests for lumber, paper, and other things, we have learned the importance of replacing the trees we cut down. In the United States, more than 1 billion young trees are planted each year.

You probably know that a forest is a large wooded area. But a forest contains much more than just trees. A variety of insects, birds, and other animals live in forests. They can be found in the tops of the trees, under leaf litter, and everywhere in between.

Squirrels and birds live on and in the trees. Mice and chipmunks hide among brush and inside dead logs. Snakes, turtles, and insects move among the ferns, mushrooms, wildflowers, and fallen leaves on the forest floor. The trees and other forest plants provide

A squirrel eats in a tree where it is safe from ground-dwelling animals.

many animals with food such as leaves, nuts, and berries. They also offer shelter from storms, strong winds, and the heat of the sun. The forest is the home of many animals. It has everything they need to survive.

We depend on forests, too. As trees and other plants convert energy from sunlight into a sugary substance that fuels their cells, they release large quantities of oxygen into the air. We breathe this oxygen and use it to carry out all our bodily functions. Without the oxygen given off by green plants, we would die.

The oxygen that all green plants give off is produced by photosynthesis, a process that converts the sun's rays into a material plants use to grow larger and make seeds. All the energy that plants need to grow comes directly from the sun.

When a plant-eating animal eats a plant, the plant's energy is transferred from the plant's body to the animal's body. The animal uses the energy to fuel its own cells, so that it can grow and reproduce. When a meat-eating animal eats a plant-eater, the energy is transferred again. So, you see, all of the energy that fuels life on Earth comes from the sun. Plants convert this energy into a form that can be used by humans and other animals. That's why forests are so important.

We need to care for our planet's forests. When a large tree is cut down, it takes a long time for another tree to replace it. Even the fast-growing cottonwood

 It takes at least 20 years for a small forest tree to replace a
full-grown tree that is cut down.

grows only 4 or 5 feet (1 or 1.5 m) per year. It takes even longer for the land to recover when a whole forest has been cleared, or cut down. Most of the time, the trees that are common in a *mature forest* cannot grow on newly cleared land.

 Only 1 or 2 years after railroad tracks have been abandoned, the land is already recovering. Plants spring up beside and between the tracks.

The first plants to grow on abandoned farmland or areas destroyed by fire must be able to live in bright sun. These plants provide homes and food for insects, spiders, and mice. Eventually the area develops into a meadow as wildflowers and a variety of tall grasses begin to dominate the area. After a few years, the meadow is taken over by a tangle of shrubs and vines. These plants give rabbits, snakes, and ground-nesting birds places to hide.

In some areas, these shrubs are eventually replaced by an *intermediate forest* of pines. In other areas, aspens or other kinds of trees may make up intermediate forests. A hundred or more years after the land begins its recovery process, a mature forest finally returns.

Each of these stages happens naturally when land is left alone—undisturbed. These kinds of changes are always happening in uninhabited areas all over the world. If you look carefully at the plants in a particular area— such as a field that is no longer used for farming, or along the sides of the road, abandoned railroad tracks, or the shore of a nearby lake, you may be able to guess how long it's been since the area was disturbed.

Eight major fires raged out of control in Yellowstone National Park during the summer of 1988.

# CHAPTER 2

## THE END IS THE BEGINNING

In the summer of 1988, eight huge forest fires raged through Yellowstone National Park. Some of the fires were caused by lightning, some by human carelessness. Because the park received very little rain that summer, the forest was unusually dry and burned quickly. In some places, the fires spread 14 miles (23 km) a day. Firefighters were not able to stop them. By the time snow put out the fires in November, almost half of the park was affected.

Wildfires are a natural part of any forest's life cycle. In fact, the seeds of some trees cannot sprout until their hard outer shells have been melted by fire. High winds and a summer with little rain allowed the Yellowstone fires to spread quickly. But there is another reason that these forest fires were particularly destructive.

When the fires stopped in Yellowstone, new plants began to grow immediately. Nevertheless, it may take 200 years for the forest to recover in some areas.

For many years, firefighters had quickly extinguished fires in the park. As a result, the ground was covered with a lot of deadwood and dry leaves. In 1988, park officials decided to let the natural fires burn. As long as the fires did not threaten private property or human life, they were not extinguished. Park officials hoped that the fires would restore the forest's natural life cycle.

When a forest is naturally destroyed by a fire, it begins to recover almost immediately. The same is true for forested areas destroyed by humans for farming, building houses, or making roads. Once farmland or a logging road is abandoned, the forest begins to grow back.

## The First Step

Daisy fleabane is one of the first plants to sprout in disturbed soil. A seed floats in on a gentle breeze and lands in an area that was recently destroyed by a wildfire. Although the seeds of some trees have already landed here, the young plants that sprouted soon withered and died. The bright sunlight was too much for them. But daisy fleabane is different. It thrives in the bright, hot sun. It grows best in disturbed areas because it does not have to compete with other plants that would crowd it out or block the sun.

Daisy fleabane is just one of the sun-loving *colonizers* that grow in a disturbed area during its first year of recovery. Many colonizers, including horseweed and ragweed, belong to a group of plants called *annuals.* An annual sprouts, flowers, releases seeds, and dies in one growing season. Some annuals live only a few weeks, while others survive all summer long.

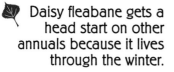 Daisy fleabane gets a head start on other annuals because it lives through the winter.

Annuals do not have extensive root systems or store extra food. They spend all their energy on growing quickly and producing a lot of flowers, *pollen,* and seeds. Horseweed, for example, may grow more than 6 feet (2 m) tall in one year. When the wind carries large quantities of ragweed pollen through the air, many people develop a flare-up of hay fever. One pigweed plant can make as many as 6 million seeds in just one summer!

Early colonizers cannot live when too many other plants are present. Their seeds may stay in the ground more than 20 years until the land is disturbed. When light finally reaches the seeds, they sprout and grow.

The seeds of many early colonizers have special adaptations that increase their chances of landing on bare ground. Some of the seeds are small and light-weight, so they can be carried to new locations by the wind. The seeds of other colonizers have sticky outer coatings. When a passing animal brushes against one of these plants, the seeds stick to the animal's fur. The

Although horseweed  makes a lot of flowers, they are so small that you might not notice them.

seeds hitchhike a ride to wherever the animal is headed. If they end up on bare ground, they grow into plants and produce seeds of their own.

If you visit a recently disturbed area during the winter, you will see the stalks of many dead plants. Most of these plants are annuals that died at the end of the summer. If there is no snow on the ground, you may also see clumps of green leaves radiating out from a central point. This is a type of plant called a *biennial* because it lives for two growing seasons.

During their first year, biennials make roots and leaves. Many spend the winter as *rosettes* of leaves that grow close to the ground, where they are protected from the weather. During their second year, biennials grow stalks with flowers and seeds. Then they die.

If you see a rosette with spines along the edges of each leaf, you are probably looking at a nodding thistle. In the summer, this thistle sends up a strong, spiny stalk that may grow up to 6 feet (2 m) tall. Big, soft purple flowers grow on the stalk. The thistle makes many little seeds that are carried to new locations by the wind.

Other common biennials include Queen Anne's lace and poison hemlock. Both of these plants have white lacy flowers and fernlike leaves. The delicate white flowers of Queen Anne's lace and the purple-spotted stem of poison hemlock make them easy to identify.

Nodding thistle is a biennial that spends its first winter as a rosette of green leaves.

All of these first settlers, both annuals and biennials, are tough plants. They can live without shade and protection from storms. They are able to get all the nutrients they need to grow, even though disturbed soil often lacks many important minerals. After just a few months, these hardy "weeds" can turn a piece of bare ground into a thriving *meadow*.

Besides plants, the meadow may contain a variety of animals—insects, spiders, snails, worms, and even birds. Butterflies, bees, and wasps visit the sweet-smelling flowers and collect *nectar*. Caterpillars and grasshoppers eat the leaves of the plants. Snails and

**19**

 Meadow plants store nutrients in their leaves during the summer. These nutrients will enrich the soil when the plants die and their bodies decay.

worms crawl over and under the ground. Bobolinks, sparrows, and whippoorwills hunt for food, build nests, and raise their young.

This meadow may only last about 5 years. As the roots of the first plants tunnel through the soil, they break it apart. This makes it easier for other types of seeds to sprout. Shade provided by the early colonizers helps other types of plants to grow. The new plants are also protected from wind and rain by the colonizers. When the colonizers die and decay, the nutrients from their bodies are released into the soil. This natural fertilizer helps new plants grow, too.

The new plants that begin to appear in the meadow may live for many years. As they grow, their roots spread and their leaves store nutrients. After a few years, they crowd out the annuals and biennials that first settled on the bare ground. In the next chapter, you will learn more about these longer-living plants and the different kinds of animals that come to live in the *thickets* that develop.

Although agaves live for decades before they make flowers, many of them die after only one season of flowering.

# CHAPTER 3

## PLANTS WITH LONG LIVES

Although most annuals live just 8 or 10 weeks, some plants may live for many years before they produce flowers. The agave, or century plant, which grows in the deserts of the southwestern United States, may live for several decades before it flowers for the first time. A plant called the *Puya raimondii* lives 150 years before it flowers. This plant, which is closely related to the pineapple, grows in the mountains of South America.

Plants that live a long time are called *perennials.* Like biennials, most perennials flower in their second year. Perennials do not die after one season of making seeds, however.

Some of the first perennials to appear in a meadow are goldenrods, asters, and milkweeds. In the summer, these plants blossom and make seeds. Although the part of the plant that is aboveground dies each winter, the roots and a thick central stem containing food stored during the summer continue to live. In the spring, the stem sends up new stalks to make leaves and flowers. Some perennials, such as Japanese honey-

 Many farmers grow vetch. They plow it under to enrich the soil.

suckle and poison ivy, have woody stems that survive aboveground in winter.

Because perennials live through the winter, they usually send up new stems before annuals and biennials can sprout. They take advantage of the food stored in their underground stems to get a head start. Most early-spring garden flowers—snowdrops, crocuses, daffodils, and irises—are perennials.

By the time most annuals and biennials sprout, perennial leaves have been absorbing sunlight and converting the energy into food for several weeks. Meanwhile, the perennials' roots have been gathering water and nutrients from the soil. Because perennials have these advantages, they usually crowd out annuals and biennials within a few years.

The perennials continue to improve the quality of the soil. Vetches and clovers have bacteria living on their roots. These bacteria break apart nitrogen *molecules* in the soil, so that plants can absorb the nitrogen and use it to build the compounds they need to live.

When the plants die, their bodies decay and release nitrogen into the soil. As a result, other kinds of plants can use the nitrogen originally broken down by the bacteria. Over time, the soil in the area grows richer and can support more and more plants.

Five years later, the meadow is gone. It has been replaced by a thicket. The landscape is now dominated

Bushes and trees grow bigger each year, blocking the sunlight and taking nutrients from the plants that live only a year or two.

by the woody stems of bushes and vines. This tangle of plants is an ideal hiding place for rabbits, mice, skunks, and snakes.

Other perennials take advantage of the better soil. After about 10 years, small trees begin to appear. As they grow taller, they block sunlight and eventually, the shorter plants die. A forest is on its way.

# CHAPTER 4

## THE INTERMEDIATE FOREST

An owl is half-asleep on a high branch of a pine tree. It slowly opens one eye and looks at the needle-covered forest floor below. A chipmunk darts out from behind one tree and runs up another. A gray squirrel dashes up a nearby tree trunk, too. It has just outrun a red fox. In the distance, a woodpecker hammers out a coded message as it looks for insects in a dead tree.

This wooded area is very different from the thicket it replaced. After only 20 years, the thorny vines and dense shrubs are long gone. They have given way to a forest of 40-foot- (12-m-) tall pine trees. These trees protect the forest animals from the sun's burning heat, the rain, and strong winds. Small animals can move easily along the forest floor, which is carpeted with evergreen needles.

The great horned owl hunts birds and mammals as large as porcupines and skunks.

It is hard for new seeds to sprout here because pine needles rot very slowly. As they pile up, it becomes difficult for new plants to grow. Chemicals given off by the needles kill bacteria that could make the soil richer.

Even little pine trees cannot develop in the shade of their parents, deprived of direct sunlight. Because young pine trees cannot grow, there are no pine trees

It's easy to walk through a pine forest because few plants can grow underneath the trees.

to replace large pine trees when they die. As a result, the pine forest will not last forever.

Although a pine forest is the most common type of intermediate forest in the eastern United States, a different kind of intermediate forest is more common in some parts of North America. In the northern United States and southern Canada, for example, aspens are often the first trees to grow in a disturbed area. New aspen trees grow out of the roots of aspens that were not damaged by fire or removed by bulldozers. Because the evergreens that inhabit these areas must grow from seeds, it takes longer for young evergreens to appear. In addition, aspens thrive in bright sunlight and on unprotected, bare ground. As time passes, however, the aspens are replaced by other kinds of trees.

After many years, the trees in an intermediate forest are replaced by trees that can grow in shade. These trees make up a mature forest. This forest is more stable than the intermediate forest and may successfully sustain itself for hundreds of years—until it is disturbed by nature or by humans. In the next chapter, you can see how a mature *broadleaf forest* is different from the intermediate pine forest it replaces.

 In the northern part of North America, evergreen trees arrive after and replace the aspens and birches.

Oak and pine trees can grow together for many years before the oak trees finally take over.

# CHAPTER
## 5

# THE MATURE FOREST

Although young pine trees cannot survive beneath taller, adult pine trees, a young oak tree may occasionally sprout up in the midst of a pine forest. Perhaps a squirrel carried an acorn into the forest, buried it underground, and then forgot all about it.

Because very little sunlight reaches the young oak's leaves, it cannot make much food. The struggling young tree may not look too impressive, but it is a survivor. It grows very slowly, but it does not die. Oak trees can live in the shade of evergreens for many years if necessary.

When an old, dead pine tree falls to the ground, the oak finally gets plenty of sunlight. It grows quickly and soon fills the gap left by the old pine. Slowly, after many years, the evergreen trees are replaced by oaks and other broadleaf trees. Eventually the pine forest will be replaced by a mature forest that contains a variety of *deciduous* trees—trees that lose their leaves each autumn.

## The Forest Gets a New Look

The oak tree that struggled for years until an old pine tree died may eventually be taller than a 10-story building. Each summer it grows a little more. Unless the oak is attacked by insects, it will continue to grow as long as it gets plenty of sunlight and water. During

After the leaves have fallen, you can see how the branches of forest trees do not spread far from their trunks.

the summer, a typical oak absorbs 150 gallons (570 l) of water each day through its roots. Most of this water evaporates into the air through the tree's leaves.

During the oak's 200-year-long life, its surroundings have changed a lot. Most of the pine trees have died and disappeared. They have been replaced by oaks, hickories, sycamores, walnuts, poplars, and other kinds of broadleaf trees. The branches of the younger trees do not spread as far as those of the old oak because the younger trees had to compete with each other for sunlight as they grew.

Although the tops of the trees get plenty of sunlight, their lower branches do not. As a result, many of the lower branches died and fell to the ground. As these dead logs rot, they provide places for skunks and salamanders to hide, for mushrooms and mosses to grow, and for termites and carpenter ants to tunnel. A hungry snake pokes its head out from beneath a log and slithers through the leaf litter in search of a meal.

Meanwhile, other insects feast on the leaves 100 feet (30 m) above the forest floor. A little closer to the ground, a squirrel makes a leafy nest about the size of a laundry basket. Birds build their nests on some of the trees' lowest branches.

Unlike the pine forest that was here before, the broadleaf forest develops an undergrowth of plants beneath the trees. The leaves of the broadleaf trees fall off

This lady's slipper is one of the many beautiful and unusual wildflowers that grows in the forest.

every year, making a richer soil where certain types of shrubs and flowers can grow. The plants that live under the trees are slow-growing perennials. They often have large flat leaves that make the most of the small amount of sunlight available.

## A Year in the Forest

Broadleaf trees make most of their own food and do most of their growing during the spring and early summer. By the middle of the summer, they are taller and wider. They have new branches and a more complex network of roots. They have also made buds for next year's flowers, twigs, and leaves.

As the days grow shorter, some leaves turn red, yellow, or orange. Soon they fall off the trees. The leaves of the old oak turn brown before they fall. Most insects and spiders die. Many birds head south for the winter.

Squirrels scurry through the forest collecting and hiding acorns and other seeds to eat during the long,

The reds, yellows, and oranges that were hidden by the green chlorophyll during the summer, become visible when the trees stop making chlorophyll in the fall.

cold winter. An average oak tree makes about 5,000 acorns each year. Because acorns are rich in protein, mice and deer eat them, too.

Life in the forest is more difficult during the winter. Since the broadleaf trees lost their leaves, they cannot make food. So they must rely on the food they stored during the summer. In addition, heavy snow may bend or even break some of their branches.

The cold temperatures and snow make it hard for animals, too. They have trouble walking through deep, soft snow. Squirrels may not be able to find their hidden stash of acorns. Instead of tasty, nutritious leaves, deer are forced to survive on bark.

Some animals sleep through the winter. Bears and woodchucks fatten up during the summer and autumn, and *hibernate* in dens for the winter. Some moths spend the winter in cocoons, while snakes curl up together in crevices between rocks.

In the spring, the forest comes alive. Hibernating animals wake up and birds return. As sunlight warms the earth, perennial wildflowers such as trillium and violets shoot up from their underground roots and stems. They grow quickly, flower, and make seeds. Then, shrubs, such as laurel and spicebush, begin to flower. Soon, small trees like the beautiful dogwoods and redbuds blossom. These shorter plants bloom before the tall trees make leaves that block the sun.

Trillium and other wildflowers on the forest floor are the first plants to bloom in the spring.

Forest animals begin looking for mates. Birds build nests and lay eggs. When their young are born, the parents spend most of their time searching for food to feed their new family. Other animals have offspring, too. The young animals have all summer to grow big and strong before they face the harsh winter.

This yearly cycle of a broadleaf forest is common in many parts of the eastern United States and Canada. The story is a little different in forests found in other parts of the world. In the next chapter, you will take a brief look at other types of mature forests.

## MEADOW
When cleared land is left undisturbed, a few hardy plants begin to grow. As wildflowers and a variety of tall grasses begin to dominate the area, the land transforms into a meadow.

## THICKET
After a few years, the condition of the soil improves. A thicket with a tangle of dense shrubs and thorny vines replaces the meadow.

## INTERMEDIATE FOREST
Eventually, small trees begin to sprout up. In many parts of the United States, the thicket gives way to a intermediate forest of pine trees.

## MATURE FOREST
After many years, the trees in an intermediate forest are replaced by trees that can grow in shade. These broadleaf trees make up a mature forest.

# CHAPTER 6

## OTHER KINDS OF FORESTS

### Northern Forests

Evergreens dominate the mature forests of some northern regions of the United States and Canada. These forests, which may be made up of only one kind of tree, can also be found in the Rocky Mountains. These are not intermediate forests. Broadleaf trees such as oaks and hickories will never replace the evergreens.

Only evergreens such as pine, spruce, and fir can endure the cold temperatures and short growing season of these northern regions. Evergreens do not lose their needles, so they can begin making food as soon as the ground thaws enough for their roots to absorb water. A waxy coating on the needles protects them from the cold.

Evergreen trees in the northern forests, like these black spruce trees growing in a Canadian forest, often grow close together.

The forests in the northeast are made up mostly of spruce and fir, while the forests in the northwest consist mostly of spruce and pine. Northern forests also have a few types of flowers such as bunchberry, wintergreen, and twinflower. These flowers cover the forest floor in areas where sunlight gets through the trees.

 Bunchberry can grow in the northern forests as far north as Alaska.

Some of these northern wildflowers have leaves that stay green all winter.

Many types of animals live in northern evergreen forests. There are caterpillars that eat pine needles, and birds that eat the caterpillars. Snowshoe hares and mule deer feed on twigs and bark. These animals are hunted by lynxes and wolves. Beavers build homes that dam streams, creating ponds where moose, porcupines, and other animals come to drink.

## Tropical Forests

A very different type of forest can be found near the equator. Here the weather is hot all year round and there is always plenty of water. Giant trees stretch to the top of the tropical rainforest in search of sunlight. Below them is a thick maze of smaller trees draped with vines. Very few small plants grow on the dark forest floor.

The broadleaf trees of a tropical rainforest do not drop their leaves each autumn. As a result, the trees can continue to make food and grow all year. That is why many rainforest trees are so tall.

The tropical rainforest has a greater variety of trees and other plants than forests to the north. Huge woody vines called *lianas* may grow as long as three football fields. As these lianas stretch upward toward the sunlight, they wrap themselves around trees. They must reach the top of the rainforest before they can produce flowers.

Many other kinds of plants live among the top branches of the rainforest, where they can get some sunlight. The roots of these ferns, mosses, and orchids do not reach down to the ground. They grow in piles of rotting leaves that form in the places where tree branches come together. They get water from moisture in the air, and minerals from the decaying leaves and

 Since tropical forests are always warm and rainy, the forest looks
about the same year round.

insects. Bromeliads also live on the branches of rainforest trees. Their leaves fit together tightly to form a cup that holds water. Insects and little frogs spend their lives in these pools of water.

Since rainforest plants grow all year, there is plenty of food for the animals that live there. Caterpillars and other insects eat the leaves of the rainforest trees and vines. Hummingbirds eat nectar produced by orchids and other flowering plants. Brightly colored parrots eat seeds, nuts, and fruit.

 An orchid's roots help it grip notches between tree branches.

Some animals have a more varied diet. Many birds eat fruit, seeds, and insects. Monkeys also eat a variety of foods. In turn, these creatures are a source of food for meat-eating rainforest animals. Iguanas and aardvarks grab insects with their long tongues. Leopards will eat monkeys, duikers, and a variety of rodents.

## Pacific Forests

A different type of rainforest grows along the Pacific Coast of North America. This *temperate* rainforest is not hot, like the tropical rainforest, but it is wet. In fact, it is nearly always damp and foggy.

The trees in this rainforest are *coniferous*, which means that their seeds grow inside cones. They include firs, hemlocks, cedars, and spruces. These trees may grow to be 300 feet (100 m) tall and have huge trunks. Different mosses grow on the trunks of these trees, and club moss hangs from the branches.

Many types of ferns and flowers can be found on the forest floor. The forest is alive with the calls of chickadees, nuthatches, and blue jays searching for food among the branches of the tall trees. Far below, deer and elk munch on shorter vegetation. A mountain lion, crouching silently behind a nearby rock, waits patiently for one of these plant-eaters to come within pouncing distance.

Winds blowing across the Pacific Ocean bring a lot of water to the foggy forests along the coast.

It is hard to believe that this healthy mature forest could be destroyed in a matter of hours—one lightning bolt could start a fire or a few bulldozers could cut down dozens of trees. Once the trees are gone, many of the forest animals will have no place to live and no food to eat. They will be forced to move to other areas or die of starvation.

But, as you have already learned, the end of this mature forest means the beginning of a wildflower meadow. And, eventually, over many years, a new mature forest will develop and flourish. This is a natural cycle that has been taking place for millions of years.

# CHAPTER 7

## CONTROLLING THE FOREST

A forest's natural cycle of growth and development will continue uninterrupted—unless people do something to stop it. Have you ever mowed a lawn or pulled "weeds" out of a garden? By cutting the grass or removing certain plants from a plot of land, you were stopping the forest at a very early stage in its development.

Besides preventing a forest from growing, people can also choose the type of forest that grows in a particular area. For example, in the southeastern part of the United States, people prevent intermediate pine forests from developing into mature broadleaf forests by occasionally setting small fires that kill the young broadleaf trees. The people who own the land prefer pine forests because pines grow faster and can be used to make paper, furniture, and other products.

If a homeowner does not cut the grass and remove other plants from his or her lawn, a forest will eventually take over.

These forests must be closely managed to success-fully disrupt the forest's natural recovery cycle. Despite human attempts to prevent broadleaf trees from growing, oaks, hickories, and other broadleaf trees often manage to grow fairly large. Trying to keep broadleaf trees from growing in these forests is as much trouble as keeping weeds out of a flower garden.

In recent years, many forest scientists have begun to understand that putting out natural wildfires in national parks and national forests also affects what type of forest grows in an area. Many now feel that natural fires—like the fires that destroyed much of

Yellowstone National Park in 1988—should be allowed to burn.

The lodgepole pine, which is common in Yellowstone National Park, is an example of a tree that needs fire to reproduce. Its cones do not open up until they are heated. Also, fire clears the undergrowth, making room for the seedlings to grow. Without fire, the lodgepole pines in this forest would be replaced by spruce, fir, or other trees.

Whether a forest is burned or cut down, it will come back. It's hard to stop a forest from developing. As long as the soil remains and there is enough rainfall, the process of recovery begins almost immediately. Within a few years, a piece of barren land will become a meadow. As time continues to pass, the meadow becomes a thicket. Once a few small trees sprout up, the thicket is on its way to becoming an intermediate forest and, eventually, a mature forest. At each stage, the land supports a variety of insects, spiders, birds, snakes, and other animals. By studying how forests develop, you can learn to appreciate their complexity and their incredible ability to recover from a variety of disasters.

 Stands of lodgepole pines grow on the lower slopes of the Rocky Mountains.

Oak

Sycamore

Hickory

Pine

# CHAPTER 8

## ACTIVITIES YOU CAN DO

These activities will help you to identify trees commonly found in forests of the eastern United States and Canada. You will also learn how soil can affect a forest's ability to grow and how observe and record forest development.

## Activity 1: Identifying Trees

Visit a broadleaf forest and look at the trees. Use the drawings on page 54 to identify four kinds of trees that are usually found in this type of forest.

## Activity 2: Comparing Soils

Compare soil from a meadow, thicket, and wooded area. Look for differences in color, moisture, and texture.

Rub the soil between your fingers. If it feels gritty and breaks apart easily, it contains a lot of sand. Plants have trouble growing in very sandy soil because rainwater drains out very quickly. If the soil sticks together and forms lumps, it has more clay than sand. But, too much clay is not good for plants, either. The water drains so slowly that it is difficult for air to reach plant roots.

The best soil contains some clay and some sand. If the soil is dark, it probably contains a lot of nutrients. Most plants grow well in this soil.

Which area has the best soil? How does soil type affect the kinds of plants that grow in each area?

## Activity 3: Keep a Record

Find an abandoned piece of land. Using stakes, mark five locations. Visit the site four times a year—once during each season. Each time, record the date and your observations in a journal or notebook. What types of plants are growing at each site? What is the condition of the soil? What types of animals do you see nearby? You may not see the animals themselves, but be on the lookout for their homes, footprints and other markings, and discarded food. You may even want to take photographs of the area and keep them in your journal.

# GLOSSARY

*annual*—a plant that lives for only one growing season.

*biennial*—a plant that lives for two growing seasons.

*broadleaf forest*—a forest that is dominated by deciduous trees.

*colonizer*—one of the first plants to grow in an area.

*conifer*—a tree with seeds in cones.

*deciduous*—trees that lose their leaves in the autumn.

*germinate*—to begin to grow.

*habitat*—the place where a plant or animal lives.

*hibernate*—to pass the winter in sleep.

*intermediate forest*—a forest that will be replaced by a mature forest.

*liana*—a large, woody vine.

*meadow*—an area with grasses and wildflowers.

*mature forest*—a forest in which many trees are fully grown.

*molecule*—a group of atoms that form the smallest unit of a substance that can exist and retain its chemical properties.

*nectar*—a sweet liquid produced by plants.

*perennial*—a plant that lives longer than two years and makes seeds year after year.

*photosynthesis*—the process by which plants use sunlight to make food.

*pollen*—the male sex cells of green plants.

*rosette*—a cluster of leaves in a crowded circle.

*temperate*—having a climate that's not too hot and not too cold.

*thicket*—an area with a dense growth of shrubs and vines.

# ADDITIONAL INFORMATION

## Books

Feltwell, John. *Animals and Where They Live.* New York: Dorling Kindersley, Inc., 1992.

Forey, Pamela. *Wild Flowers.* San Diego: Thunder Bay Press, 1994.

Forey, Pamela, and Cecilia Fitzsimons. *An Instant Guide to Wildflowers.* Stamford, CT: Longmeadow Press, 1991.

Goodman, Billy. *The Rain Forest.* New York: Tern Enterprise, Inc., 1991.

Hamilton, Jean. *Tropical Rain Forests.* Parsippany, NJ: Silver Burdett Press, 1995.

Hickman, Pamela M. *Habitats—Making Homes for Animals and Plants.* Reading, MA: Addison-Wesley Pub. Co., 1993.

Kochanoff, Peggy. *A Field Guide to Nearby Nature: Fields and Woods of the Midwest and East Coast.* Missoula, Montana: Mountain Press Pub. Co., 1994.

Lawrence, Eleanor, and Cecilia Fitzsimons. *An Instant Guide to Trees.* Stamford, CT: Longmeadow Press, 1991.

Peterson, Roger Tory. *Peterson First Guide: Wildflowers.* New York: Houghton Mifflin Co., 1987.

Petrides, George A. *Peterson First Guide: Trees.* New York: Houghton Mifflin Co., 1993.

Royston, Angela, ed. *Trees of North America.* San Diego: Thunder Bay Press, 1994.

Whitman, Ann H., ed. *National Audubon Society Pocket Guide to Familiar Trees of North America East.* New York: Alfred A. Knopf, 1995.

## Multimedia CDs

*The Amazon Trail.* Minneapolis, MN: MECC, 1994.

*Destination: Rain Forest.* Redmond, WA: Edmark Corp., 1995.

*Smithsonian Presents: Total Amazon.* Simon and Schuster, 1995.

## Organizations to Contact

National Park Service
United States Department of the Interior
Washington, D.C. 20013-7127
(202) 343-6843

U.S. Fish and Wildlife Service
United States Department of the Interior
Washington, D.C. 20240
(202) 343-4131

U.S. Forest Service
United States Department of Agriculture
Washington, D.C. 20013
(202) 447-3957

# INDEX

# ABOUT THE
# AUTHORS

Robert Mania received Bachelor's and Master's degrees from Michigan Tech. University and a Ph.D. in Physics from Virginia Tech. He has taught at the college level for 16 years and is presently teaching physics and math at Kentucky State University. He has also worked with middle-school children who are advanced in their studies. During the summer, he does research for the U. S. Army, Navy, and Air Force. Robert has written computer reviews for *PCM Magazine,* contributed to two science exam books, published eleven articles in technical journals, and prepared more than thirty U.S. government research laboratory reports.

Cathy Mania graduated from Morehead State University with a degree in math and chemistry. She also has a Master's degree in higher education. She has taught high school and college students. Cathy has had several poems published and exhibited in two art shows, including the 1996 Expo in Frankfort (Kentucky). She is currently majoring in art at Kentucky State University, and is a member of the Capital Area Art Guild.

Robert and Cathy live in Frankfort, Kentucky with their two children. In preparation for this book, they visited state and national forests in Kentucky and Virginia. Many of the photographs and illustrations that appear in *A Forest's Life* were provided by the authors.

11/02
8/04·2
6/06 - 4